Screaming

BLACKNESS

LET THE CONVERSATIONS BEGIN

Ronald May

Aka Jitwala

Dinah May graphic artist creation of the cover.

Rich Book Business Publishing -Coaching
www.richrelationshipsus.com
ISBN: 978-1-7357018-7-5

PUBLISHING & COACHING

DEDICATIONS TO...

My three sons: Brennan May, Ryan May, and Bradley May. Thank you for the encouragement from son to father. One of the accomplishments on my "Bucket List" was to have a close and meaningful relationship with my children. The memories of you three as children always warms my heart. I look forward to the adventures and conversations we will have now that you're adults. I'm blessed to have each of you to grow and flourish with.

Dr. Norman Chambers, my Psychotherapist, who became my dear friend and mentor. I met you as a college student and I'm a better man because of it.

Seidric Tapscott, Kasimu Harley, my college roommates, brothers and friends for life. We will always be brothers. Screaming Blackness is as much a part of you as it is of me.

Reynold Bryan, James Daniels and Marvin Anderson. Three dear friends that I can always depend on. My thoughts and beliefs need challenging friends. You guys always saw my point and raised me a point; kept a brother on his toes.

I shared my vision to write this book with my son Ryan. I asked him what he thought about my idea for a book. Ryan replied:

"I believe your book will be of help to someone's life one day."
-Ryan May

INTRODUCTION

My goal in writing this book was to create a catalyst for positive, progressive conversations and thoughts surrounding Black identity and cultural evolution. As a baby boomer, I have watched America change in profound ways and remain stagnant in others.

I am encouraged by the sense of unity demonstrated by our community at this moment in history and I would like to add to the conversation. It is important to keep our history alive, to remember our struggles and traumas, and recognize their manifestations in the present. However, a purely retrospective approach to understanding Black culture leads to the retracing of our predecessors' footsteps rather than building on their progress. This retrospective approach to understanding our people and forming our cultural identity requires a healthy, positive dimension for us, individually and collectively, to actualize our potential and lead progress-oriented yet fulfilling lives. That current, future-oriented, self-focused conversation is what this book hopes to encourage. Perhaps members of other cultures can also use this book as a lens for understanding Black consciousness.

Contained in this book are a collection of my 'Poetic Thoughts', compiled throughout my life and each is paired with a "Pragmatic Theme". The passages after each poem are meant to illustrate my mindset when the poem was written and my purpose in sharing. The poems themselves are meant to inspire your own creativity and ignite your humanity with thoughts that are unique to you.

My hope is that readers of this book will share it with those close to them, exchanging their individual insights with one another. Culture is defined from within and ours will continue to evolve with our collective understanding. From my heart to yours. -Ronald T. May

TABLE OF CONTENTS

GROW OLD

(College Student, 1974)

Grow old! You Black man.

Grow old in a world where few Black men have grown old.

Grow to know and reflect thyself--

Yes, grow old you Black man.

Passing down a heritage of which you have only felt

but have never truly seen.

Manifest! You Black man.

Make tangible the ideas that disturb your mind

but never forget to grow old.

Dig deeper, into your comic thoughts and realize that they
can change the world,

If made manifest.

Pierce deep into your forever and try on a world that fits.

Yes.... Grow old, You Black man.

Change his-story, to my-story, then read

Grow Old! You Black man

with your feet in history.

Convicted to the real world,

The changing world, the growing world.

Yes! Grow old, you Black man

BUT...

Never

Ever

Be

Afraid

To

Die!

GROW OLD

Just how does a parent with natural, loving feelings toward their child preserve their innocence, while teaching them potentially psychologically damaging information? This is the dilemma many Black parents find themselves trying to navigate. Generations of parents have strived to teach Black children their methods for positive living and daily survival techniques in a society with a racist history; a racist history that just won't die. The lessons taught throughout the generations include explaining that your life could be sacrificed, to make one of several points. Lack of equality in America could be a point. Another point could be a demonstration of superiority that White Terrorists, calling themselves some form of Supremacists, keep trying to make.

This poem, *Grow Old*, written while I was in college in 1974, is not about any psychological concepts such as Learned Helplessness. It's about the unyielding essence of life that makes it possible to survive everything but death itself.

It is this essence that allows us to survive and thrive day-by-day, year-by-year, and generation-by-generation. It also prepares us to demand equality, equal justice, and an accurate portrayal of our historical and future contributions. Our ancestors were brought to this newly developing country by force. They had no safe method of self-expression. Those who spoke up, even slightly, were horribly maimed or killed, until all the normal, overt attempts at resistance, stopped out of consequential fear. Somehow, our dignity still survived, so that your hands and minds could one day be completely untied and we could have our voice and freedom of expression; giving us and our future generations the opportunity to "Grow Old".

This poem challenges us to look around and examine our existence. If the only thing you perceive is catastrophe, confusion, and ineffectual rebellion, then you do the sacrifices of your ancestors a grave disservice. These sacrifices should encourage you to do better, for the sake of your future freedom.

The poem, *Grow Old,* aims to pass on a more fruitful reality to your next generation's loved ones. Help them grow old, by creating loving and safe homes, and nurturing neighborhoods with a self-defined culture that is forward-oriented and one to be proud of.

Early America stole fulfilling life, even longevity, from us. Therefore, we have an obligation to reclaim and restore that life for ourselves, using our own cultural and political images, with our own instinctual understanding. God put a talented tenth in every cultural population for this purpose to be the thinkers and the cultural vanguards for the people of that culture. When you hear the more accurate truths from our leaders, it will ring true to something inside. A sort of truth bell. That's the thing that Dr. King spoke to. He made elderly people proud to walk during the Montgomery, Alabama bus protest for 381 days. When asked, "Aren't you tired of walking?" They said, "My feets are tired but my soul is resting just fine". They understood the sacrifice of their ancestors and the value of sticking together. You must strive to be astute enough to understand that our cultural and political life goals are achievable. However, we must never forget to grow old.

THE ESSENCE OF LIFE

(College Student, 1975)

How can I tell you of the essence of life?

When you have it... you will feel it.

When you have it... you will breathe it

and with each breath, the sacks of the lungs of your mind

will fill hopefully, with the essence of your life.

You'll need not be reminded to conform
to the necessities of your progression

and you will care not about failure.

For the knowledge learned from failure

will only more pave the road to success.

Just how does it feel

to know that you walk in rhythm and in harmony

assured that you are living for your purpose?

It feels Spirited.

It feels wholesome knowing that each and every part

Fits exactly the way that it was meant.

But as I write, I lose the thoughts;

Lost in reaction to my capitalistic born fears

and I struggle to regain.

My fears close the briefly open doors;

Doors open for brief moments

when I am able to see the thin lines, between society and life.

Brief moments, when I am God:

Creator of my existence, assessor of my future

and benefactor of my past.

But as always and with great agony,

The thrust of society

with its concrete knowledge

Overwhelms my desire to pursue the abstract

And I fall bitterly into the perpetual existence

of what men call society.

But I must learn and I must express

For with knowledge of truth, I remove bond after bond from
my beautiful mind.

Beautiful not because it is mine

But beautiful

Because it can see and know life

and realize

That with knowledge of truth ...

I... Can. FLY!

THE ESSENCE OF LIFE

The *Essence of Life* was written in response to a spiritual argument I was having with my God. God oftentimes requires of us, a level of patience that is difficult to follow. At times, I believe that we've all asked God for our own personal "Burning Bush", something clear and concise, without all the biblical explanations and confusions. Confusions coming not because of any lack of pursuit into God's word but coming because of our diligent pursuit into God's word. How can your study be wrong and the studies around you be so right?

The *Essence of Life* is a wonderful poem. It flowed out from me in one piece, almost like it just needed to be scribed for presentation and edification. Its spiritualism touches the lives and hearts of many who have already heard it. Spreading its glory whenever and wherever it's being shared.

The poem, *The Essence of Life,* is itself a talking burning bush. However, the poem was revealed without revelation and meaning at the time it was written. I didn't realize it was the answer to my questions of God in my life. The revelation came to me when the poem *Essence of Life*, was ready to reveal or maybe when I was able or ready to receive it. Life really knows no limitations regardless of your circumstances. Circumstances are conditions that we can strive to overcome. Life's only limitations are the ones we put on ourselves leaning on our own understanding.

Victory, failure, and even tragedy can be the forces behind your successes or failures. If there is a yearning inside you, follow it. Mold it daily, until it becomes your reality. That is the Essence of Life, as I see it. I have always sought my own biblical understanding and that has been my struggle at times, and my guiding light at others. Find God for yourself. He said, "If you ask with a spirited heart, I will reveal my message to anyone". I've learned to lean on that understanding as I've pursued my "Essence of Life".

LIGHTHOUSE
IN THE GHETTO

(1978)

If we had a lighthouse in the ghetto--

Then, all our ships lost in the daylight hours

Could find their way home.

If we had a lighthouse in the ghetto;

A lighthouse that shines really bright--

So, those lost in the daylight hours would not
still be lost at night.

Ghettos toss and turn,
can suddenly turn showing an ugly face;

Then, it can mellow and turn to a sweet lovely,
neighborly place.

It's safe to play in these moments,

Not sure it will last all day.

Don't worry about tomorrow.

Today, you jump, skip, hop and slide.

For now, come out little children, it's safe to play outside.

Poverty's an enemy, from birth until we die;

Moving out of the ghetto, can save so many of our lives.

If we had a lighthouse in the ghetto,
It could teach us each day
To not boil your life down to just trying to get paid.
Communities die- your son, my daughter, our children
can't safely play outside.

Look! There's another small one dead, shot in the head
By a bullet that had no eyes.
You hear the mothers crying,
You see the neighborhood crying, too.
You didn't know them personally;
They lived maybe over just a block
or maybe they lived over two.

Why did they have to die?
'Cause someone pumped their chest to get respect
And shot the bullets that had no eyes.
That's a fact: who you shot in the back
was a kid playing outside!
Now you're on the run because you pulled a gun
And shot a bullet that had no eyes.

There is no lighthouse in the ghetto.

There's just the lighthouse of our minds.

Use this lighthouse wisely,

When your anger starts to define

Or you'll lose the respect you thought you'd get

Shooting the bullets that had no eye.

LIGHTHOUSE
IN THE GHETTO

There's a beautiful place in La Jolla, California where I would go as a college student to be alone with my thoughts and take in the gorgeous view. I'd sit on this giant rock in the early evening and watch the tide come in, bringing bread with me to throw to the ever-present seagulls. Several of them would fly speedily after it, with the winner grabbing it and veering in a sharp arc at the last moment, avoiding collision by the breadth of a feather. Somehow, they never truly collided.

I loved this place and I'd stay for hours, spellbound by the view of the ocean and the soft sounds. As the tide came in, the waves would hit the rock I sat on, reverberating with a bass like tone and sending a giant fan of water spraying into the sky. The glint of the sun's rays would produce a gorgeous rainbow amongst the drops. This would happen over and over again as I laid on my back and enjoyed myself.

One day in particular, I was feeling disturbed and looking forlorn out into the beautiful scene produced by the body of water. My gaze drifted aimlessly, eventually landing on a lighthouse that was just off the shore. My thoughts meandered onto the purpose of a lighthouse, how they warn ships of rocky danger and offer light for guidance and safe passage. While watching the lighthouse, my mind wondered, "What if we had a lighthouse in the ghetto that could guide us towards safe passage, making our lives better and warning us of impending dangers and pitfalls.

Many such lighthouses already exist in the form people that love bravely, embodying self-sacrifice for the sake of improving our communities. They are intrepid enough to question, "What's always been and why must it be that way?" Always looking for and finding solutions and discarding darkness to illuminate Black lives, beliefs, and ideas. These thoughts birthed the poem *Lighthouse in the Ghetto*. The line in the poem that resonates with me the most says, "Then, all our ships lost in the daylight hours could find their way home" ... If we had a lighthouse in the Ghetto.

SOUL'S GOT E

(College Student, 1975)

I am survival but there was no movement in me.

My heart has been hardened down for so long

and my eyes refuse to see what they might

But my soul has got ears that hear crying
from a thousand years ago.

Who knows better than I how it feels to cry that ancient tear?

A tear that does not slither down your face.

A tear that's caught; caught in place, in your eye.

A tear that's been forming for so long,

You can pluck it and put it on a chain

and, oh they'll exclaim,

What an interesting thing you wear!

What does it mean?

But cry out, cry out,

I hear your words, your words so clear.

For you see, your soul has got ears

that hears crying from a thousand years ago.

Soul's Got Ears--

Ears that always hear.

For there's no control greater than the will of your soul.

Black man, Black woman why you look down?

Raise your head and look around.

Hey... I know what you are doing.

You, that ancient soul,
tuned in on the latest version of pain is here to stay.

So, Cry Out, Cry Out, that silent message that rides on air,

"We Shall Overcome Someday"

Who knows better than I?

How it feels when
life's background music is whips and gunshots

and move nigger move.

But let me tremble, let me tremble old ones,
because I too now understand.

I am strong and will always carry on,
but we need this small tremble

and the drop of the ancient tear
that so long been around our necks.

So, Cry out, Cry out, when all seems lost,

For you see

Your Soul has got ears.

Your Soul has got ears

That hears crying
From a thousand, thousand, thousand
years ago!

SOUL'S GOT EARS

The poem, *Soul's Got Ears*, echoes of our roots' past, present, and future. The love for a past that needs to be remembered and requires expression. The poem shares the humbling privilege of unity with our ancestors that desire their lives to be remembered and shared for the benefit of the universe and American Black people. It is an ancient spirit that cries out its message.

Imagine the agony of the people in the Middle Crossing on tightly packed slave ships. The cries of millions of African citizens thrust into this tear-filled journey who died while desiring and trying to live. The survivors and those that died wanting their past world not to be forgotten or their devastation ignored.

Some loving spirit prompts us to carry this message of the "Ancient Soul" that still loves and caresses its generational offspring with cultural honor and presence. Honor this message, Black People. The message from a faraway land, time, and culture that still lives untainted in its ancient forms, now and always will. Our combined hearts are strong enough together to carry and live the messages from a thousand years ago.

The core of a people's existence is language, culture, and symbols that define their earthly past, present, and future. Suddenly, it's gone and it needs to again be found, for in you its good lives and wants expression. The Black American's entire assemblage of the cultural symbols we held dear for generations were destroyed, yet, somehow there exists a connection to my ancient ancestors through this poem. If you just, at times, quiet all the noise in your life and just focus, your soul can and will hear their messages. Their cries are our desires that are riding on the ancient winds. The wind grabbed their cries long ago and carried them safely on the sacred spirit that cannot be killed.

Our sacred spirit, however, you define it, brought us through our holocaust and will continue to do so as we become whole. If we just stop and listen, we will realize that the same spirit loved you then and it loves you now. All we need is love and respect for our collective self because our Soul's Got Ears that can hear crying from a thousand years ago.

SINGLE MAN

(College Student, 1976)

As a single man,

I know as a single man.

As a single man, I express myself as a single man.

I can yell, I can tell, and if said too loud, "Bang!"

I may end up in hell

Because I am a single man.

As a double man,

I believe as a double man.

As a double man, I converse as a double man

I can yell, I can tell and if said too loud, "Bang! Bang!"

I may end up in hell

because I am only a double man.

As a triple man,

I feel as a triple man.

As a triple man, I bite as a triple man.

I grow.

As a group,

I ask

And I am heard.

SINGLE MAN

What can you do to affect your circumstances in America all by yourself? NOTHING! Just go and holler in the woods when you are all alone, you get nothing other than a release of your individual frustration and emotions. Your eloquent or explosive release of self-expression is wasted on an audience of trees that will not understand or in the case of some people, will choose not to hear you at all. You're just speaking into the wind.

Accuracy and clarity in profoundly stating facts doesn't matter much either if you are a lone voice hollering for changes in an established institution. You might just be considered crazy by some and considered a hero or genius by others; however, you're still a lone voice that's misunderstood and may be considered dangerous.

Unifying behind cultural adaptations won't provide any real relief either. Sagging pants, alternative language styles i.e., Ebonics and isolationism provide egotistical sanctuary but have no political value in a land governed by laws and political and legislative strategies designed to effectively obtain control over you.

Let's stop fighting amongst ourselves and embrace the political processes required of sophisticated people who understand how this system functions for and against us. Without committed political understanding and trustworthy leadership of our own choosing, our agenda items will never see the light of Congress. This is how it is when we strive for our specific rights in a Constitutional Republic. As a single man, I am only a single misunderstood voice but as a group, I ask and I am heard.

BLACK AMERICA

(College Student, 1976)

My dream was not dreamt
For I heard it just the other day.

My dream was not dreamt
For I see it every day.

Can it truly be my dream?

My dream is dreamt for no one knows it.
My dream is dreamt for no one sees it.
And as my dream unfolds, new to all,
Someone will say, 'Look that's nice'
and it will be...
But I'll know that it's my dream.

BLACK AMERICA

Black Americans have always fought, wished and prayed for America to live up to the promises it makes to all of its citizens. There are plenty of Negro spirituals ringing throughout our history that express our yearning for a better day. We all know them from going to church and maybe some marches.

We also embrace Dr. King's speeches, which tell of this better day and a "new founded faith". But why a "new faith"? Because the old faith, when our voice was not represented by any of us at the table, is severely tainted! Faith was purposely suppressed in us to limit our humanity to that of servitude, maintaining an aristocracy that excludes people of color, by God's ordaining (according to some), from the essence of America's dream.

Still, we dreamed anyway, with persistence, step by step bringing our dreams closer to reality. Some of our advancement has truly been a byproduct of the larger social interests. For example, the Union did not fight the Civil War to right the wrong of slavery but because it could not afford to allow the South to emancipate. Still, as a consequence, our freedom took a giant leap forward.

As we move forward, actualizing the Black American dream, may we creatively find ways to drive progress, both within and outside of the system. Equality and citizenship don't mean forgetting who we uniquely are. It's demanding our contributions be respected and accurately portrayed in the country we helped to birth and build and fought and died for. Others will never paint our picture accurately, so we must. A nation whose philosophy allowed for a Black woman to breastfeed a white child but required public drinking water fountains to be segregated cannot and will not paint my reality accurately because of the foundational belief of racial superiority that can only exist because of racially legislated laws.

LIFE AS I SEE IT

(1977)

I try to live life as I see it and I see it all.

I see the dead and the living.

I see the loving and the giving.

I could die happy.

I could go to the mountaintop

or I could live in the sand.

I could part with an arrow.

I could swim with the seals;

I could lay with a gorilla and love how that feels.

I could run with a leopard

and dance all on the beat

As my toes ache, I would love it--

For it, all would be unique.

Is there a heaven? Is there a hell?

Is there some way to tell?

The sky is love and mine to delight.

The ocean is wisdom and it shines day and night.

The grass is mine to lay and relax.

While fingers of air, scratch at my back,

While I slowly simmer

To feel it all is my dream come true;

To be it just once, that's my dream too.

How can I tell you? What can I say?

The Lord looks over this everyday earth, in His special way,

and the earth beckons and it calls

With beauty profound--

Enjoyed by the knowing;

Feared by the weak and dared by the strong.

If I could tell you, if I could tell you in words that were clear.

If I could show you in a picture, that's flicked by a gasp.

If I could give you directions, or show you a map,

Then, I'd be the man that history says

Now and then stops off to love.

But I'm of this life, and at times, it is so clear

That the clear life:

The life I should hold very, very dear--

That's the life that my heart is taught to fear.

LIFE AS I SEE IT

Stubborn is the stolen mind of Africa's mothers. Stubborn, yet, confused trying to live a lie to stay alive; to understand realities that don't fit with my capabilities. There's nothing I can't do.

I'm given essential tasks daily while being told about my inferiority. My ideas manifest all around me but I will no longer be allowed to live if I take credit out loud for what everyone knows I did. That's life as I'm told to see it.

My eyes can see the truth, my heart bursts when my thoughts become realities and my genius makes life easier for all and more lucrative for others. Yet, from time to time, I must make the time to just enjoy my life in the center of all these contradictions. Everyone can feel what life should be about. The phenomena of a powerless people tells us that an oppressed people will try to assimilate and mimic the oppressor: a task Black folks were unable to do because it wasn't just a simple name change for us. Our skin color just stood out no matter how accomplished we became at playing our designated social role. If we were Lowdowski, Bernstein, or O'Reilly, we could just drop the 'ski', 'stein', and the 'O', we would be instantly American.

Certain nationalities were discriminated against because of their country of origin and religious backgrounds. One of the first times America closed its borders to immigrants was to keep out Irish Catholics. They were immigrating into this country in massive amounts and were changing the political and religious dynamics of the country. They certainly saw their share of Irish Not Allowed signs. The point is we, as a people, must define for ourselves how we want to just be. Much of our social interaction has been reactionary to avoid racist hostility. That can no longer be our primary motivator.

The Black Lives Matter Movement is birthed from this thrust to rid this country of what has been termed Systemic Racism. Systemic racism is under attack by Americans that are young and upcoming and by decent folks that don't want that reality any longer. It's a shame it's taking this generational change to bring about a more decent America but the inbred reality is, it has.

Black Americans have long enjoyed the successes of accomplishment in this country. We've accomplished, sacrificed, died in defense of this country and on and on. This has not deterred the conviction of racists to keep white people as the advertised owner of our society. I do believe change is coming because old racists are dying and the American people are searching for real answers to the declining lifestyle of all non-wealthy Americans.

White Americans voted for Donald Trump looking for answers and only the worst racists got their dreams answered. For a short while, they got to feel superior again and express it. Parading around the Second Amendment guns and holding racist rallies with this country's President. What did the majority of Americans get other than empty promises and a country that's currently an embarrassment worldwide? The unexpected racist culture consequence of a xenophobic President hasn't made America better and we all know that now.

We shouldn't need a Black Lives Matter Movement but we do because systemic racism exists. Its continued existence allows for unprovoked verbal, violent, and lethal attacks by some of America's citizens and the police on Black American citizens. Let's keep working towards a citizenry that's for the people and of the people. Then, we can all live our lives as we see it.

FOREVER YOURS

(1977)

Forever yours, for a part I am.

Born lost in a world where lost has no hope.

Born a man, dreaming a dream, that only I hear.

Born with the knowledge to know

But too foolish to believe.

My eyes blinded by the things that I see

and just cannot believe.

My heart hardened by the things that I feel

and just cannot relieve.

I cry... a grown man's cry, at the age of twelve.

My heart yearns to feel

But reached out

Snaps back... singed a thousand times.

I find the world around awaiting me

To engulf my very soul.

My purpose and my true reasons for life.

I travel these roads though--

For strong I am

Searching to find what is truly mine

and I find

Me!

FOREVER YOURS

Across this country, we are intricately connected through the Black Experience. The journey of relieving oneself of the various forms of internalized anti-Blackness is never a straightforward process. It requires intellectual trudging through misrepresented facts and history, as well as introspective navigation through complex, socially reinforced norms.

As Black Americans, we live in a world of duality, requiring a kind of "cultural centering" that we need but is somewhat difficult to define. Our citizenship, though legally concluded, is riddled with inconsistencies. The same Constitution that freed us from slavery, was once used to enslave us. Principles of patriotism lie in contention with our experiences of oppression, as even the most upstanding, illustrious Black citizens are not immune to systemic prejudices and systemic racism. As things stand, the promises endowed by citizenship still do not completely extend to Black Americans and navigating this reality is often both intellectually and spiritually challenging. However, Black Americans have managed to cultivate and define an ever-evolving culture, in spite of a surrounding environment that attempted to snuff it out. "Remember Black Wall Street", should be a mantra, a rallying cry.

The journey towards continued cultural evolution requires the renaissance of a "National Village", where we offer support to each other as we strive to reconcile the irreconcilable. It begins by finding love within yourself and sharing that love with others. That's why I call you "My Brother" or "My Sister". Others have asked, "Why do Black people greet each other so often in passing?" The answer is simple: Adversity breeds fellowship.

I, THE WINGED BLACK MAN

(1979)

I, the winged Black man, go not care where.

I fly up to heaven and soar down to this hell;

Yet, one from the other, I cannot tell.

Captured and taken through the vastness of their seas;

No understanding of what futures are in store for me.

I know my home's rivers, I know of my home's seas;

Always the giving waters were friends, a source of life for me,

Then the waters brought the xenophobes on ships

Without warning the people of my race

Were herded on ships headed to some unknown place;

Chained down, not able to move, breathing
in each other's face.

Life fades, time passes, while heading to this unknown place.

Will this nightmare ever end?

Will I ever see my home, my loved ones again?

I thought of my village around the baobab tree;

How it's deep roots will always keep its secrets for me.

It has strong branches where I would sometimes sleep.

To think of the great tree gives me despair,

It's there forever, but I am no longer there.

I know nothing of this new place.
My old home grew love, this place raises hate;
I feel the hate all around.
My eyes get me punished for looking up or straight ahead,
So, I just look down to avoid the dread.

Somehow, someway I'll live for tomorrow;
I endure these evil days for those that follow.
Yes, I, the winged Black man, go not care where.
I fly up to heaven and soar down to this hell;
Yet, one from the other, I cannot tell.

I, THE WINGED BLACK MAN

Can we as Black Americans make our own sense of the grand dream that carved out the culture of this place, we call America? It's not real and yet, its realness affects our daily lives. America is a group of sayings and platitudes that resounds to the rest of the world about a place of hope. A concept that ideologically exists, but realistically doesn't.

America was founded and formed first by the annihilation of the Native Americans. Followed by an invitation to people migrating from everywhere. Some seeking fortune, many seeking refuge from abysmal circumstances, and some just plain thrown out of their country of origin. Everything these assortments of migrant people believed was weaved into this "American Ark", shaping the development of this country. Unique people from all over the world with varying beliefs from every culture strived to forge an existence preserving their cultural values while attempting to coexist or assimilate into a larger cultural context. That is, except Black folks and Native Americans whose lives were sacrificed to facilitate and provide the foundation of this country.

Black people's roles were to be socially invisible, while effectively working under dehumanizing conditions as an essential labor force. We hovered just below citizenry, seeing but never actually being what our contribution should have afforded us. If you look closely and accurately, we laid the foundation for every step in America's progress, without sharing in the prosperity. Thrust into this strange reality, we became the "Winged Black Men" functioning in this society without a place to land and call our own. We were given a concept of heaven to embrace as we lived our imposed hell. The Winged Black Man became our survival--a way to cope with being necessary, but unwelcomed; alienated but managed closely enough to be useful when needed.

PASSION

(1978)

Why must I, in my life

Have so many times of stress and strife?

I learned at a young age, the arts of glee

But the practice of them soon did not satisfy me.

Yes, there were volcanoes erupting and star spangles galore

But something inside of me said, there had to be more.

Just what was it for?

For pleasure, for fun, for me, for you, or just to be done.

Sometimes I sit down, and Lord do I think

Of the sustenance, I wasted on Holiday Inn sheets.

We grunt and we grind

and through these means, we try to find

Our manhood and our womanhood

and we make seals for life.

But be careful young man that...

that passion does not become your wife

For problems will kill that passion

and that once exotic Dove will fall to the ground;

Pierced through the heart by your missed shot love.

Now, do not despair

and trip out your life,

But learn to control yourself

and to pay true love's price.

Because the kinds of feelings

That you want, need and desire to feel,

Those kinds of feelings will only come when they're real--

And you can keep them safe because your love

This time is for real.

PASSION

I n the Black community, like many communities, manhood is often measured through sexual exploits. This dynamic is poisonous, as it compromises the wonderful beauty that exists in genuinely affectionate, intimate romantic interactions.

What effect does having multiple passionate but loveless sexual encounters have on young people's emotional development? If you are seeking and can healthily navigate such interactions, do your thing. However, attempting to substitute genuine affection with the physical embrace of the arms of a stranger has become a consistent and damaging norm. You've had every sexual experience a person can ask for, yet never really knowing or caring to know any of your lovers can leave you yearning emotionally. If you've never felt the yearning for more from a person than just a great orgasm, perhaps you will one day, and I hope you do.

Creating quality families is a requirement to keep our communities strong. We cannot do that if the premise of "Baby Daddy" overcomes the premise of "Baby's father" within the context of family. The consciousness of our communities should not have terms like "Baby Daddy" as a substitute for "Father".

I hope this poem prompts you to consider that and want more than passion from sex and more than Baby Daddy labels from your relationships that produce children. It is especially detrimental to our community development to leave a string of children without consideration for their livelihood or relationship with their lineage. If you just have children and they do not carry the last name of their biological father, they will not know their lineage with consequences that would be tragic for any patrilineal culture.

Young men, have some women in your life that you like, respect, love, and yes, even adore. Have someone you can cultivate a real friendship and loving romance with, along with all the passion. If all you know how to do is chase physical pleasures, no matter how proficient you are at your sexual exploits, that hurts you, your children, the many women you'll encounter, and the healthy development of the culture we seek.

HAVE YOU EVER TRIED

(1980)

Have you ever tried?

Have you ever tried to lift this weight with your Blackness?

Have you ever tried to look through all of this madness?

Aware I became, of this awesome game

and determined to be a man,

I developed my own master plan.

My plan took me through hell

Because at any time, I could have ended up in jail;

But at that time, all that I knew

Was a game called, 'Yes, I'm Smarter Than You'.

I twisted this way and I twisted that way;

I planned out my strategies

and then I began to realize

That the "Man", he was planning stride for stride with me.

So, I sat down and I started to think.

My understanding said, "This game is not that deep

Cause I saw Howard Hughes on TV

and he was just another creep.

So again, I rearranged and to my mind new ideas came

But most importantly, I saw that my game
was not new at all...

Because every time, that I wanted to see me,

All I had to do was turn on TV.

And there I was black and down,

Dressed in high-heels and listening to sounds;

And waiting for something to fall my way

or always looking for a better game to play.

The brothers told me, Ron, come and get high

And when I relaxed, they tried to pick my mind.

Now, I cannot think of why it took me so long to see

That the only one that I could really listen to was me.

At this time, the world was all a glow.

I saw red people. I saw white people. I saw black people.

Hey, I even saw some Negros!

Mine was the whole wide world

and although, I personally had never been,

I still saw myself as an international man.

Yes, I walked around, and I strutted without fear

and out of the masses, my world began to appear.

This all seemed so great, my body always tingled

and I stayed ready to debate

But something inside, would always make my heart hesitate.

And then...
And then, from somewhere in my past;
A past much older than I,
My greatest ancestor appeared and he took me by the hands.
He slapped me down to my knees
and said, "This nigger you are now, you will no longer be".
I said, "Who are you talking to, with your dead ass?
Great, great ancestor, from my past.
He reached to his eyes and pulled out some tears
and he laid them on the ground.
Visions of things, I've never seen, began to dazzle, all around.

I looked in those tears and I grew to know
That there was no such thing as a ne-ga-ro.
But from out of those tears, I was forced to come
and now more than ever, I knew I had no place to run.
I had to look at myself and what I had become.
Yes, I watched and I waited, for this all seemed so new
and it seemed so serious, what I had to do.
But the struggle had begun
and me, being that basic man,
I cast those illusions, given to me, by another man.

So, if you read my poem,

If you hear my poem

and to you, it seems somewhat clear.

Then, that means that I have passed along the love

That my heart holds

So very, very dear.

HAVE YOU EVER TRIED

Have you had times in your life where conflicting ideas and concepts just plague your mind? For example, college is an environment where the constant flow of diverse informational perspectives can be a bit unsettling to a young or untrained mind. You have your views that have been with you throughout your life and suddenly, or not so suddenly, your views get challenged or expanded requiring consideration for change and self-growth.

These can be very precarious times for a young person on their own trying to figure out for themselves their beliefs and direction. The directions you can take are many and varying. Rhetoric whirls around you and you may not have the discernment to know the difference between unproductive avenues that shouldn't be followed and productive ones that should. You can be easily influenced by what makes sense at the time and that may very well turn out to be a mistake. This is especially true when someone you respect eloquently presents their perspective to you with their best interest at heart.

Dr. Shirley Thomas, a professor at San Diego State, once said to me, "Understanding and evaluating new ideas and beliefs is the essence of the educational process. You do not have to consume the ideas and live them in order to understand them. You must choose how they fit in your grand plan before you implement them. Take time and do your own due diligence."

Many young folks get in over their heads before they realize the full implications of their decisions. Take your time to thoroughly understand if these changes you are considering are good for you, your future, and your direction. Develop relationships with mentors that you cultivate at a pace you feel comfortable with. Real mentors will help you find answers after you've exhausted your own understanding.

Looking for answers to your curiosities can be a wonderful process. Always evaluate any knowledge from multiple perspectives. When information makes you feel better on your journey it still needs to be intimately understood before you allow it to become a life direction. Read about it, talk about it, and proceed with the caution of your evaluation process.

HEY BABY, I'M GONE

(College Student, 1978)

With time ahead and my future not clear,

I can only go forward, although you've made my heart stop.

Where did I fall? What do you want?

I gave you all that I have, I kept myself only for you.

Allowing my temple to only be touched by you.

Sometimes when I'm all alone, I used to sit and play:

How my future would be with you, a game I truly enjoyed.

Now, I'm sitting and faith in myself is all I have, once more.

Sometimes, if not for hardships gone by,

I would like to lay down and die.

I see you now in my mind, having the time of your life

And even from these images, I draw some joy,

For I'd rather see you here, than not at all.

Yes, lady, you had my heart, my soul and my future plans.

You brought out in me, in a few short months,

What America has taken centuries

and billions of dollars to hide from me.

I am so glad that the qualities of a Black Woman

Cannot be manufactured.

Even now I sit, eyes watery, but the pain refuses to come.

As I've always tried to tell you,

I know the game but I thought in you

I had found a throne upon which I could sit.

I thought in you

There's a place that I can take out my heart

And put it on display, for all the world to see.

When we were together,

I actually concentrated on making you happy

and realized a strength that I didn't even know was there.

You may not even be able to accept it but I loved you.

But because I am also a lover of my life and happiness--

Hey baby, "I'm Gone"!

HEY BABY, I'M GONE

Feelings about everything can get scrambled when an undying, forever love goes bad. I don't know if there's a good way to tell or be told that feelings you thought would span eternity have changed. There may be some compassionate ways of doing it but there certainly are a few ways that it should never be done. However you lose your love, especially your first, it's going to hurt you in ways you didn't know you could hurt.

What do you do with this kind of devastating emotional pain? There are effective ways and ineffective ways to handle yourself during these times. Handling pain "well" is relative, as it's not really something you can directly resolve. It's persistent by nature and passes when it's run its course and no sooner. You must wait, cope as best you can, and take as much solace as possible in the knowledge that things will get better.

There are slews of responses you'll consider. Some will get you put in jail and some can turn your life into a living hell. Your desires dry up and life will seem empty and maybe even hopeless. Young people often laugh at the notion of a broken heart. Though for most of us, it has at one time or another been our reality. Trust me, I do know of which I speak. It's a shame that most young people won't understand how truly devastating a broken heart can be until the first time their life's energy is sapped from it. Truthfully, this is when many young folks start to grow up, have empathy for others, and stop telling sweet lies, with false intentions. They begin to realize for the first time that someone's heart is nothing to play with.

Recovering from hurt is part of maturing and becoming a caring person. While you can enjoy the romantic opportunities that your looks, personality, or abilities may open up for you, try to give your love only to those that know just how precious love is, how to respect it, and how to take care of it. Also understand, you are not exempt from a broken heart. The next heart to be broken may be yours, and then you'll truly understand the meaning of this poem.

This poem is about a great love with a selfish person. One that took love for their own fulfillment without consideration for the other.

Here's some advice specifically to those falling in love: Sometimes it is best to listen to your intellect's assessment of a situation, even if it goes against the desires of your heart. There are times when you must do what's best for you, regardless of your emotionality.

STRAY BOY

(2018)

The stray boy is now on the run;

Scared to death because life stopped being fun.

No real player skills, he's not from the streets--

Never had any reason to survive;

No need to steal just to eat.

Quickly made a name with those born of the streets.

Raised with beliefs to just work hard--

Keep your ass out of the streets;

Never go out of the yard.

His parental protection stops giving directions

As young and old collide.

Some of that stuff son, I forbid you to try

But no explanation did the wise ones provide.

Ongoing battle hurts your father's pride.

He's just trying to control his son's steps,
so that he doesn't die.

Making sure there is no early heaven, no early hell;

The boy might just have listened if the father didn't yell.

The boy is a young man that cannot be just told,
'Cause you raised him to be strong;
You made him be very bold.
You figure now is too early to try things on his own
and you'll put him out of the only home that he's ever known.
Neighbors know he's been told by you to go.
They hear the street drums beat
and they ask why is this one living on the streets?
Why is he not home?
He's too nice, too young, to be on his own.

Warm strangers warn him of the danger of youthful pride.
They see the puppy's eyes are not yet opened wide.
Young, naïve, filled with pride,
He still has trust shining in his young eyes.
There's pain, fear and boldness, where there was once joy.
Life's twists and turns will change this young boy.
Tales and talks of not being worthy
Have sent this young man on this tear-filled journey.
He took his life in his own hands
When he made his first stand.
And said to his dad, I am a man

{53}

His dad told him to leave now, if you think you're a man.

No North star to follow, no railroad underground;

Not sure what in the streets will truly be found.

With the strengths given him by a good home.

He'll find out about life's ways, all on his own.

Hunger sets in and he feels the pain;

Nothing learned in school will kill hunger pains.

The disagreements that would not allow him to stay.

That made him put on his Jordan sneakers and sneak away

With his car, some clothes and really no cash.

You pretty much threw him out with the clothes on his back.

Like a scared scarecrow and a wolf in full bay,

He makes the lonely sounds of those that stray.

Life-drops, like raindrops, will fall tonight.

He and you sit and wonder about who's wrong, who's right--

It's hard for you to go to bed

Wondering where your son is tonight;
where will he lay his head?

But none of those thoughts will feed him tonight.

The criminals and people of the street will teach him to fight.

Somehow, someway he will take his time;

He's determined to find a way to eat without doing crime.

He has it inside him to know right from wrong.

He knows because you raised him to know

This is not where he belongs.

But he has to adhere to the calls of the streets--

Right now, for a place to sleep and something filling to eat.

Days pass until at last

Life lights the way and he sees a path.

With nothing to lose, he played in a game;

Someone saw him and wanted his name.

They needed a player and when they found

That one of his caliber was just hanging around,

This stray boy is no longer in the streets--

Because he took his time

and learned to eat,

Without committing crimes.

STRAY BOY

What's it like for a young person discovering they must fend for themselves at too early an age? Maybe they ran away from home, just walked away, or were asked to leave. However, it occurred, they've left their first home because they can no longer live there. Perhaps you're a college student that no longer has the family's financial support. A recent high school graduate or a young person just released from jail or the military. However or why-ever you are on your own, you're now on your own. You find you will need to make decisions about the values you are going to live by. The paths you choose from all the options have to now be chosen by you, and not only be guided by your circumstances.

Think hard about what you want out of your life before you ruin your future with short-term thinking and decision making to just fulfill your immediate basic survival needs. Don't be so naïve that you allow yourself to get into trouble not of your own making. When providing for yourself is a daily task, there are always temptations that can lead you down paths that can ruin your future long before you can really get started. With some planning and some practicing of patience, life has ways of providing assistance out of the worst of situations. There is something to be said for just having patience and working at living decently.

Short-term solutions and temptations are alluring when you're young, broke, and on your own knowing hunger for the first time. Do you take short cuts, to care for yourself? You can always sell drugs, rob folks, steal, break into houses, hoodwink women, or any number of clandestine life arrangements that might feed you or possibly will get you arrested. Many of your friends and acquaintances in and of the "street life" will call you a fool for believing in a better day. They have all the answers and they also have the police records to go with all their wisdomless beliefs.

Try being in the group of "Stray Boys", in the streets working towards your better day. Keep your dreams even when you cannot see how you can possibly achieve them. Sometimes persistence is all you have. The streets will teach you how to survive, mostly on the dark side of life. Making honest daily survival money is not going to be easy but it can be done. Don't be above making an honest dollar. Needing daily money is the reality you've gotten yourself into. Give yourself an honest chance to achieve something better than hustling every day. Which way your future goes is truly up to you and the choices you make while you're a "Stray Boy".

YES, BLACK PEOPLE, WE'RE HEAVY

(1980)

Yes, Black people, we're heavy but we're not ready.

Have we consumed the needed knowledge?

Have we realized the difference when
we seek out and actually go to college?

Do we know ourselves from the world
or are we still confused?

Do we try in vain?

Has this unique culture so locked us in our chains

That we cannot see our own culture? Use our own brains?

Anyone thinking there is an America is a fool;

For they will wait forever
for America to play its philosophical part.

Anyone thinking there is no America, is a fool;

For she'll smite you down

If you forget the realities of her heart.

Yes, my people, we're heavy but we're not ready.

Is the reason for our struggle apparent to you?

Or are you still trying to figure out what to do?

Do you see our struggle as black and white?
Or as a discussion to determine who will control our might?

Our might?
Oh silly are we to talk of something
Not yet to be!
Our might is the struggle of a plant,
Breaking through concrete to feel the warmth it lacks.
The warmth of unified consciousness,
the ease of mind of protection,
the sense of pride of destination;
the determination of purpose.
Yes, my people, we're heavy but we're not ready.

I see the black youth movements they are now trying.
They speak of black life mattering
with no commitment to dying.
But die we do,
While the criminal justice system hides truth.
We lie in the streets--
Choked, scared, and beaten by the police.
In a cowardly act',
A black man running and was shot in the back.
A nine-year-old boy playing with his toy gun;
Shot by the policeman who had a real one.

Civil and black progress fades, again laid to rest.

How many more black people

Will have their hands undeservedly lain cross their chest?

Lynchings used to happen in the dead of the night;

Now black lives are taken while

Cell phones rolling under bright movie lights.

Our growth needs the strength of boldness;

Not more spiritual chatter.

Black lives and life since slavery have always mattered!

The black lives matter story grows cold,

If each generation shines up the movements that have
already been told.

Listen and learn the history as it is told,

Truthfully by the ones that you call old.

Your youthful thoughts glisten because

you didn't listen or bother to look

at the information that we wrote down in our books.

You've taken to a ground already plowed,

By the death and suffering of your great grandfather's and
grandmother's child.

They hit us with bottles and bricks;

Spit on us; hit us with sticks.

Through all that we gladly fought

so the next generations
would have the privilege of their own thoughts.

So, if the Black lives of old matter to you

and I believe that they do--

Add dignity, have respect for those that came before you.

All things matter in our cultural lives

If what we want is for
the Black Lives Matter movement to thrive and survive.

Yes, my people, we're heavy but we're not ready.

YES, BLACK PEOPLE, WE'RE HEAVY

The ongoing debates defining and redefining the problems and solutions Black people face in America are generationally endless and somewhat unchanging. The more we try to culturally mainstream into America, the longer the list of challenges grows. Unfortunately, this is true even for those Black Americans who believe they have insulated themselves from Black American realities because of their economic status or personal achievements. Their list is still daunting; it's filled with a different set of problems and solutions because money cannot buy racial equality in this hierarchy of color world we all live in.

Living the historical and cultural lies of societally based inferiority vs. superiority to define social norms is at best demeaning and confusing. Yet, somehow there has always been those people, whose spirit cannot be silenced. We have our churches, our righteousness, our Civil Rights techniques--past civil rights versus the civil rights techniques of modern day.

Still, just what are the best paths to follow to achieve some sense of civil contentment? To just be able to be based on your abilities? Should we vote with or live by a set of rules that has promised to address our pursuit of equalities but has fallen short on execution? The disenfranchised grassroots intellectuals eloquently capture the essence of the Black problem, present a workable solution, and finalize with verbosity and inaction.

The Black elders' disagreement with the emerging youth's leadership, determination, and direction creates another stream of debate and conflict. The youth leadership want to deal with their life realities. Many of them didn't grow up needing "The Dream". They are the fulfillment of Dr. King's message and are being asked by the elders to slow their roll. Sometimes it seems as though the rhetorical debate has become the reality as the pleas for Black unified action fail to be implemented.

Equal protection under the law is a perfect example. Yes, there are those that will do any despicable thing to keep America's separate and unequal past alive. They want this country's past to again be their reality. The question is, how will your actions help ensure that America continues progressing for all Americans more equitably? Yes, Black people, it's one thing to be "Heavy". It's another thing to be "Ready".

THERE COMES A TIME

(1980)

There comes a time…

In life when we realize that we don't know.

When the dreams, hopes and aspirations held dear, fall;

And there appears reality,

When all that you've ever known is wrong.

A time when confidence is all that you have;

A time when tears fall the full distance

and splatter against your feet,

Or your eyes drown when upward your gaze is cast.

There comes a time…

When neither of the four directions hold hope.

When the words of the greatest singer won't stir you,

Or the innocence of your child goes misunderstood.

There comes a time…

In all our lives when we want to shake from head to toe;

Rearrange our very souls

And say, 'I too know!'

There's a time...

When friends won't understand.

When hurt seems natural

and marriage vows have turned into the latest rap.

When lovers cease to love.

When your only real possession
is the ground on which you stand

and it changes with each step.

There's a time...

When all of life weighs heavy

and you can't see

How one weight carried by so many

Can burden any one individual.

There will be a time...

When the world around glows clear;

As the light of illusion dims

and outlines of reality appear as your mind adjusts.

A time when no longer, will you think you know;

No longer will illusions hold you still.

A time when the birth of life makes you glow

and the warmth of my hands will register hot against yours.

A time when my heart will
beat through the air and stir your blood.

A time when my anger will circumcise reality.

Mine knows not the restraint of 'I can't',

or the truth of 'It's just not that way'.

Mine cares and wants care; mine loves, and wants love

Mine hurts when I don't even know your name.

Yes, there will be a time...

When all our hopes will be ours.

When dreams start from birth.

When grown men won't act like babies

and babies can be young.

Yes, there will be a time...

When hot will turn on cold.

When the icy paths between you and I will melt into a river

and we will flow towards a greater understanding.

Yes, there will be that time...

Mine is the process that helps when you're down;

That consoles when you need

and only consoles because you need.

There will be a time...

When the stars that are loved are the dim stars.

When a, "May I help you," is sincere

and you have faith that my smile is for real.

Yes, there will be that time...
Shined brightly
'til it's once overpowered essence shines on reality itself;
And on that day, we shall rejoice forever!

THERE COMES A TIME

Irony produces agony for the Black lives struggles of America. The deceptions that have been sewn into our psyche keep us confused about how to be whole fully functioning citizens of our birth land. Accepting how diabolical this country's plans were (and are still this day), is healthy for Black Americans. It makes you play Chess in life, instead of Checkers.

A real irony for Black Americans is we have to live here because America is our home. It has been from the time we were made captives and forced to cross an ocean to a tragic reality. That tragic reality has morphed in many ways because this is, in all actuality, a land of laws supplemented with amendments through positive legislative acts like the Emancipation Proclamation, the Civil Rights Bill, and hate crime legislation. Through legislation much has changed. We also can contribute many changes just to the passing of time and generations.

The racially tainted truths of our American Black history were so devastating to any happiness, contentment, or just simple dignity that for years we dreamed, and still do, of being part of the land we were stolen from. A land that in all reality has become foreign soil. Anywhere on the continent of Africa is culturally unknown to us. Those dreams, of belonging to the lands of our ancestors, may never be realized. For most of us, that ship sailed on a one-way trip unless we can afford to return as a visitor with a visa.

Dr. Karenga, the creator of Kwanzaa, says that all men should be in charge of the daily destiny of their own lives. That means dreaming a dream that can actually be realized. He also teaches that if a people's culture is stolen and replaced by another's ideology, especially one designed to deny them basic dignities, they have the obligation, and right, to create a culture that is more conducive to the actual pursuit, of life, liberty, and family happiness. There is a 'talented tenth' within every population of people obligated to design, create, and advance a culture that is representative of that group as the chosen people. The goal of our vanguards is the achievement of cultural actualization within America's present and future history. The true story of our people can then be accurately written and shared by us.

The story of the Black American contribution written about truthfully improves the American tapestry. Our rightful place in history, told truthfully, makes this a greater country. Black Americans can then contribute even greater contributions, unencumbered. There are contributions like that of Dr. Charles Drew, a graduate of Columbia University. He was a Black American physician that developed ways to process and store blood plasma. Also, there was Katherine Johnson, who was directly responsible for the success of the very first and subsequent American crewed space flights. These are extremely significant contributions that Black Americans accomplished even while encumbered with racial inequality. There are many other Black American contributions that have gone shamefully untold. Therefore, on the power of racially editing history to tell a false story, my mind is very clear. Just remember, there comes a time...

GET UP NIGGA,
YOU AIN'T DEAD

(College Student, 1977)

Get up Nigga, you ain't dead!

You, like that hummingbird

That just done lost some of that hum.

Man, we should be humming and humming!

The girls and the guys are lined up getting high.

The girls looking good;

Showing plenty of hips, large booties
and sweet gorgeous thighs.

Let me take your pulse and see if you are still alive.

Stop role playing the past, rehearsing your life's lies.

Do that every day and your life will keep passing you by.

Drop that philosophical hurting mess;

Start looking at the ladies in the short, short, red dresses.

Let's you and me, go home, get sharp and don some attire;

Then let's set these lovely black sisters' whole world on fire.

I know your losses were back to back to back,

That's enough to knock anyone off their track

and make them just lie there in pain;

Never giving or trying love again.

Facing life's pains is never fun.

It hurts just like your eyes do

when you look straight into the sun.

With the easiest of smiles comes the surprising pain

of using muscles that will make your face smile again.

It's been awhile since your face felt the rays of the sun;

You've been like a hummingbird that lost all its hum.

Now, listen very closely so your mind can get fed,

Life moves on even if you lay there acting dead.

Trickle, Trickle, Trickle--

Eye water drops and turns into cold icicles.

Heads bow for the ones defined as Black...

Get Up Nigga, You ain't dead!

GET UP NIGGA, YOU AIN'T DEAD

From time to time, there are things that just take you out of the groove of being a cool, calm charming individual. Known about town, admired for the person you are; however, in this world, there's an unlimited number of situations that can rock your world. Leaving a lethargic mess where there once was this totally together person. Loss sometimes just stops your world from spinning and takes away your joy. Now, you're in this crazy place where wonderful life is still all around you, you're just not participating. You're watching your life watch and wait on you.

Your long-time tight, tight friends, who will stand by you through thick and thin, are getting a little tired of all your moping and demeanor of devastation. They know the hurt has got you right now. You mope along and they mope right along with you. The only music you can stand right now is the Blues. Then one day your friends will just grab you up and say, "Enough"! "Snap out of it; 'Cause you ain't dead and we are not going to watch you pretend to be dead anymore".

The point is hurt and pain are very real. If you want, believe, and expect sincerely, you can be deeply disappointed. That's just how life is. Look forward to that day when your heart will soar again because you allowed your hurt to run its course and you're all good again. 'Let's go set the world on fire'. Get up Nigga, You Ain't Dead!

FIRE-BARREL
BLACK BROTHERS

(2019)

Fire-barrel Black brothers

left the homes of their heart-broke mothers.

All left broke, now homeless,

'Cause their life choices
were filled with their selfish coldness

That left them all living just a step above homelessness.

Living like worker ants,

Waiting once a month for their government food stamps.

Some have nowhere to be.

Many have lost the love and trust from their families.

They ride on the girl kids' bicycle toys.

They took the bikes from the girls,

'Cause they couldn't take them from the boys.

Living under the sky--

Hoping for a way to get high;

Needing something better when the sky's not dry.

Refusing to live not wanting to die, lie, cheat

and steal just to survive.

Most are quick with their mouth;
They talked so much, they got thrown out the house.
Now, they don't need to pay rent,
'cause they ain't got a red cent.
But it's a good day 'cause they smoked a fine jay--
Always discussing world events.
"Shoulda" put soap on the rag
to wash away the funky scents.
Know it alls, with multiple flaws;
Wearing the same dirty clothes,
wearing the same dirty drawls.

Never or always dreaming,
Always willing to do some kind of scheming.
Wishing they could find a woman that needs pleasing.
Love's not their way—
just need a place eat; if lucky a place to stay.
Out on some hustle, chasing money everyday;
Now distraught 'cause they just got caught.
For a few days, the county will pay and then a public defender
Will boot them on their way,
After attaching a probation bill that has to be paid.
Believe it or not, this goes on every day.

FIRE BARREL
BLACK BROTHERS

I t's winter and very cold outside. You need somewhere or something to help beat the chill back as evening comes on. Fortunately or unfortunately (depending on your perspective at that time), you settle in a place attracted by the light from a lit fire barrel providing light and warmth for this night's comfort. The warmth of a lit fire barrel attracts all kinds of seekers. It could someday very well attract you because of your current circumstances. You're now among the people looking for a night's comfort with strangers that don't mind them being around for the night.

Tonight's entertainment might be the new guy or the old guys telling the same old tall tales and lies. Starting with topics like, "I used to be", "I once was", "The White Man", "Do you have" or "Can I borrow". Maybe it's just two people that are currently having an issue that can accelerate into something violent very quickly. All these "street situations" are starting material for tonight's unusual enlightenment.

Those who live around fire barrels talk about making money more than most millionaires do. Probably because each little bit of money helps feed the desire for food, drugs, or tobacco. Money is gotten from doing odd jobs, thievery, hustling, stealing, or whatever else allows a few dollars to be made for that day. Sometimes, a treasure trove may be an ashtray full of long cigarette butts. The same person that made you split your side in laughter, just a second ago can, just like that, become your adversary and get his head split open or split yours open over the smallest infractions. Still the night, like time, moves on. Whoever still has any left, takes the last of their particular intoxicant while watching tempers occasionally flare up and down.

People need a place to warm their hands when they have no home to go to anymore. Maybe they just need it for now. In fact, they may have several fire barrel spots they wander between, working to become part of those who are welcomed when they show up. If they can't finesse a welcome, they move on before it gets to the state of unwelcome and someone just might get hurt.

CRACK PIPE

(2017)

When the Crack pipe really messed up your life,
'Cause you'd sell you, or anything else, for a hit on the pipe;
Because all you know is what's happening now
Because the pipe kills all your dreams and
Those of your wife and those of your child.

Your child's life started with a hit.
The one the baby got feeding from her momma's loving tits.
She knew she just bought a hit of Crack
From the money she may have made wiggling on her back.
Instead of spending it all on Crack,
She could have spent some on a baby formula called Similac.

Because you're on "Crack"--
This choice for you was not truly yours;
But now you're in a lifestyle that sometimes makes you
whore.
For drugs and favors, you live the life of a trick.
The need for crack in your life
has straight men turning gay tricks
You never know just how far down you will go.

Keep thinking you can control Crack and soon you will know

You're playing with disaster of everything you are or can be.

So, keep your eyes on this Cracker Jack prize
and you will learn, the Crack's ABC's just to survive:

A is for ass,

B is for bootie,

C is for that cracked out thot that is no longer a cutie.

Crack pipe done messed up your life;

Destroyed the life of your kids and your once lovely wife.

Now, this poem has told you what to expect;

When you finish reading it,

Put the pipe down and run to some help.

'Cause the crack pipe will screw up your life.

CRACK PIPE

A wide array of drugs has come into the Black community. (I won't spend any time discussing the politics of why.) Crack, however, was a drug, not like any other. The crack pipe high is extremely addictive. It seems to directly attack moral character almost immediately. It is extremely addicting because the "high" you're looking for is contained in the 'hit". Think about that for a second. When you finish taking your hit on the glass pipe or "Glass Dick", as it is often referred to, the essence of the high is finished also.

An immediate craving ensues and has you wanting, needing, and willfully seeking more. The craving is so strong and constant, that a Crack Head will consider doing anything presented to them for a hit that is readily available. Many argue that the "Crack Head" status will never be them until it is them. There doesn't seem to be a level of self-degradation too low to stoop to when you're crack binging. The scary part of this drug is how easily it can turn moral men and women totally contrary to their beliefs while they're under the influence of Crack. The absolute worst stories of good people temporarily degrading themselves have been 'while they were on crack stories'.

Crack was the drug that was devastating the Black community. Our community leaders asked the state and federal legislatures for help getting crack out of our communities. This plea lead to the creation of Three Strikes Law that led to the incarceration of many African American men and women for minor drug possession and not crack offenses specifically. This was an unintended consequence of our request for help. Who knew that the racists in law enforcement would use this community plea to wrongfully incarcerate Blacks with very long sentences? That's another story.

All I can say is leave this one completely alone if you must do drugs. Some people are able to deal with crack, most cannot. It takes an immediate hold on some. Many say they got addicted on the first hit and it quickly ruined their life. No one really knows why crack captures some individuals so totally. It's just known, that for some, its effects quickly take complete control of them.

Are you willing to take the chance that you might be one of those that crack just loves? Not me. I'll pass and I recommend you not take the chance either. Don't take this gamble with your life and moral integrity. Our community, your family of loved ones and your future are at stake.

I'VE GIVEN MY BLOOD

(1981)

I've given my blood until it's was almost gone,

Trying to tell what's inside, I know to be the truth;

But because it's inside and some secrets to life are unknown,

No one will really listen and the truth dies alone.

Then, life's journey showed me at last,

The truths of my future, the truths of my past.

The more I learn, the more questions I need to ask.

I want it known, written historically by those like me;

That I am a black man that was forced to cross a sea.

Origin stolen, forced into a God-awful past;

It has taken forever to become an American

Of African origin, with an African American past.

Is this the best it can be?

Tainted, unrealistic history
with no real realities of good done by me.

I've listened from birth to versions of this loving oppression;

Heard speeches burdened
with capitalistic greed and racial aggression.

I listened again and I grew to understand

That I will always be judged, just not fairly,
for the man that I am.

I can be shot dead for just taking a stand

or while running, standing, just raising my hands.

My anger now matters and I do realize

That shooting a black man, whenever,
gives some policemen pride.

These days I have to go strapped;

The second amendment is also on my side.

My country is making strapped required

To just go for a walk and I come back alive.

My blood, to turns cold, for I am told

This is what I must understand,
if I want my Black life, to grow old.

I worry daily for the young and the grown

Just going for a walk. Will they come back home?

Will a simple stop end up in dread?

When my kids are out for an evening,

I'm uncomfortable in my bed.

When I see their headlights and hear their door key,

I know now, it's ok for the parents to go to sleep.

I'VE GIVEN MY BLOOD

S ometimes, the Black movement can be so taxing that it feels like you are in constant turmoil about which path to follow. All Black folks are vanguards of the saga and future directions of Black America. The perspectives about the Negro to Black man saga in America has been completely examined-- past, present, and future. After all, understanding the problems we live with every day is paramount to change. Or is it?

Many of our leading advocates for important issues, like equal protection under the law, have a firm hold on why this is important. The actual unified direction to bring about change seems to be what is up for debate. There continues to be civil rights activists' movements, among varying groups, that push and pull and go nowhere. This poem points out our obligation to appreciate these vanguards of our cultural directions.

People who chose to speak out regarding injustices in the land of the free and the home of the brave are often unfavorably characterized as un-American, communist, and other such nonsense. Doesn't the first amendment guarantee and protect this right? "Kneeling" to protest the daily injustices of the criminal justice system is a straightforward protest. It's only about one issue: stopping the shooting of unarmed Black men. "Others", because of their desire to maintain unfair controls, attempt to change or control this single narrative. Trying to make it about disrespect for the flag or the military comes as no surprise.

This is a very common tactic designed to dilute the effectiveness of this protest. What is surprising is how many Black people miss the point and 'help' "Others" change the narrative and cause confusion amongst our ranks. There are many racial injustices that should be universally recognized and fought against by the entire Black population. Even those whose economic circumstances have placed them above this fray. Yet, we continually criticize our own attempts to expose the injustices, thereby, aiding those that want to offer a divisive narrative and inadvertently hurting our own causes effectiveness.

Respect those who have given actual and metaphorical blood for and to our causes. As Black Americans, we need to embrace and support those who have put their lifeblood into the equality game.

IT'S REALLY NOT ME

(2019)

Haters and supporters have gotten stupidly bold.

These next four presidential years may really bring tears.

To those who believe they can openly express their hatred

or impose on me their unwarranted fears,

I'll not close the doors
to my soulfulness and creative expression;

My cultural expressions need addressing
from all four earthly directions.

Worldwide, the Black man's labor was spread.

Those not willing to allow it, were usually found dead--

Hung by the neck, shot in the head;

Killed for just a look or just for something thought said.

Lawful civil rights laws give me expression

to recover culture, education,
family identity, love and direction.

There was a time when yours was always right--

Winning because you set up an unfair fight.

Telling lies, you knew weren't right,

Hoping I'd believe them...become confused

and not demand to use my constitutional tools.

How angry can you be?
Our constitutional Bill of Rights
says you have to now compete with me.
If you thought for one moment, you'd surely see
You should be focusing on the greed of the rich
and not so much on me.
The powerful use of legislative tools
to ensure the rich get richer, constantly altering the rules.
The poor, working and middle class, can't yet see
They're losing their power and lifestyle to the rich.
Their problems are not little old Black me.

You're not black! You're white!
The foolishness you believe about me and your life
Won't stand the scrutiny of daylight.
Your money disappearing
wasn't something Black folks can do.
We don't have the power to overprice schools,
To collapse the housing market, right in your face.
Give CEOs bonuses just for closing the place--
Steal millions in pensions from folks just like you.

They disenfranchised me, now they're disenfranchising you.
Your home is in foreclosure. What will you do?

You can't run and you can't hide.

You'll move your stuff; maybe you'll have to sleep outside.

Get sick. What will you do?

Without Obamacare,
there's no affordable health insurance for you.

You, self-proclaimed superior Americans,
have been such fools.

The rich now got you looking
for your forty acres and one mule.

Black folks have heard these political lies so many times;

Voting was supposed to end waiting in colored or black lines.

Keep believing trickle-down economics--
will get your wealth back

Thought you were so superior; had it all, you worked so hard.

Now, you're standing in a food line
with your EBT food stamps card.

Anyone in these lucrative days is a fool

If all you want is food stamps,
forty acres and a government mule.

Quit focusing on me as a source of your pain

,   or only the rich will rejoice,
"When America Turns Great Again".

IT'S REALLY NOT ME

The rich and powerful define superiority as personal power, wealth, political control, and ownership. Many average White Americans believe they have the inalienable right to the American dream just like the wealthy. No one dreams to be poor, yet, most are. Ninety percent of the wealth of this country is in the hands of ten percent of the population. The genius of the American political and legislative oligarchs is to promise everything and deliver the least possible that they can get away with, without causing civil unrest or outright rebellion.

The one thing the poorest of White Americans seem to cling to is their sense of superiority to people of color. It doesn't matter how uneducated, poor, or devastated their lives are. The belief that they are better than the best person of color, and Black people specifically, sustains them more than any need to fairly share in the wealth of America.

Poor Whites will vote against their own best interest. Allowing the political system, owned and manipulated by the wealthy, to tax away their chances for a better life. How can any non-wealthy citizen vote against a living wage, while corporate owners and politicians, vote in, and give themselves million-dollar bonuses? The Trump administration's latest tax legislation for the wealthy brought this out very clearly. Oh yeah, there is that rhetorical promise that the second round of tax cuts will be for the middle class.

Trickle-down economics has never worked for the poor. It just allows for more corporate stock buybacks. This makes the stock market appear to be rising. When eighty percent of the wealth in the stock market is owned by ten percent of the population, how is the rise or falling of the stock market a big deal for people who marginally participate in it? No controlling power is ever going to willingly give up power, money, or control easily. Poorest of Americans, especially in the southern states, are trying to live a past that has simply passed away. There are a lot more poor and impoverished white Americans whose plight is not very promising than there are people of color in this country.

It's ironic that what keeps you from voting in your own best interest for things like the Affordable Care Act, free two-year college, and the minimum wage increasing to a living wage is a belief that it might assist people of color. Your desire to continue to have an unequal playing field slanted in rich white folks' direction, hurts you also. Racial superiority propaganda pays the rich while it keeps the southern states having the worst economy, low performing schools, and poorest wages in the country. Where's the common sense for superiority in that?

MOUNTAIN OF FEAR

(2015)

There stands this White mountain of fear and pain.

No, it is not snowcapped.

Try to climb it, believing that we're all the same.

It's really not yours;

It's really not mine.

It belongs to the now space.

It belongs to the now time.

With the strength of my unknowing soul,

I lasso the White mountain and try to grab hold.

My mind knows not the beast that's at the top;

I tremble as I go; I've come this far, I know I can't stop.

My soulful lasso breaks, I try to escape;

I know not of this world. Have I made a mistake?

Life is made tougher for those defined black.

We did start out with chains on our minds,

With the weight of slavery drawn on our backs.

Tears flowing on the inside, the mask gets tight.

Manhood rejected;

Black women and black children pay the price.

Then, there's this voice--

Speaking so clear

That it can raise the dead, if followed without fear.

By blind faith we follow:

Onward we tread;

Then, shots are heard and our leaders fall dead.

We scatter for cover, not caring where--

Some turn into church souls.

Some straighten their hair.

Some minds stop thinking.

Many hearts break.

Some turn to anger.

Some turn to hate.

Some turn to violence.

Some try on love.

Some say, "War" and kill the white dove.

Some minds get twisted.

Fists get tight

and blue rage flows all throughout your life.

Then, comes morning and clearly we see--

This fit of despair all around us did not have to be.

What did we win burning down our own community?

{93}

MOUNTAIN OF FEAR

There are racially specific events that occur in the lives of every African American that should disturb every race of people living in the American spectrum. Throughout our existence in America, we are forever asked to put aside our understandable ingrained distrust for the chance at some sort of citizenship equality and equal justice. We are continually asked to believe that this back and forth historical debate about the abuse of our civil liberties will this time be permanent and lasting in the hearts of our fellow man. Yet, take just a brief pause from your distrust and your penalty may be slight or some profound loss because you tried trust.

Our message for equality is always eloquently or radically stated. Then we go back to the corners of our lives in America and wait. Wait again for the truly ugly realities of our country's treatment of its Black population to be uncovered completely this time, be undeniably exposed and eradicated. After all, our forefathers also died defending the country from all foreign and domestic invaders. The affronts, aimed directly at the human dignity of Black people, should no longer have to be tolerated, if the creed of America is to have any meaning at all.

Black people constantly live in a state of flux. Always on the hidden sharp edge of racial uncertainty, that defies factual explanation. If Black folks get too much equality, racism will rear its ugly American head once again. Our properties, businesses, and communities have been destroyed because they were too nice or too successful for Blacks to have. Publicly demonstrating the powerful bigoted side of the unwritten American Creed, "We must keep them in their place". Yet, when the need is there, because of some crisis, suddenly we're all in this together as Americans.

Black men depended on that when they fought bravely in the Civil War and World War II. The unwritten creed side of America rewarded their contributions with a significant upswing in hangings, reminding Black soldiers of their "place" in this society. Anti-lynching legislation had to be enacted to stop it. The American flag, by these bigoted standards, could no longer stand alone, according to these beliefs. Old Dixie must wave directly under the American Flag, sometimes above it, or Old Dixie, at times must fly alone, as a reminder.

After the newest wave of crisis subsides, Americans will once again watch their favorite media news sources for the explanations of why the unrest. The 'why' is always the same. Life in America became too intolerable for the most downtrodden of the population. Far too much harm came to the lives of Black folks. The lies and promises could no longer hold back the passion and it flowed over the racially built dams.

DEL RIO BLUES

(2017)

The room grew dim as in we all came.

The dark rays from our combined bodies

Beat down the white light.

Our minds shot out at the single source of our hostilities

and their lies could not compete.

All grew silent, and watchful, as one began to speak.

But the real problems laid
dormant amid personal confessions.

They sought not our cause

but only to relieve their personal transgressions.

The knowing grew sick and angry,

Observing these ploys of unrighteousness.

Tensions grew.

The best direction to go, no one in the room really knows.

I knew, and so did they, that nothing said was real today.

The problem remained captive, screaming to be freed.

A wasted opportunity

that could have been useful,
started to bleed and die unresolved.

How to say, in a military way,
"I am somebody" and I'm not heard.

I see. I feel. Yes, I dare to dream.

I was shot at, just like you, and it wasn't a dream.

Must there be penalties against me for no crime committed?

For knowing enough to feel when I'm wronged?

I reject the payment of penalties for knowledge unknown.

You, the white light,

Unable to compete as the black lights unite.

Forced to listen, for the room has grown dim.

We are soldiers just like you.

I feel your fear of me and I don't understand.

I am a soldier like you and I am a man.

Just as you see my hostility and appear confused--

It clears up, if it's realized; I again won't be used.

Your thoughts of me have lost their false appeal.

I now prepare--

No longer will we stay over here,

While others bathe in glory over there.

Be it known, our time and blood truly did also flow.

As darkness sets, we prepare for

This fight that takes us from here, to change over there.

'Because yes, I too am prepared.

DEL RIO BLUES

Laughlin Air Force Base is in Del Rio, Texas. Del Rio, Texas is 150 miles of desert from the nearest city in three directions, in the fourth direction lies Via Acuna, Mexico. When I returned from Okinawa after 18 months, the United States Air Force sent me to Laughlin for my last year and a half of military duty. There seemed to be a decision to send a large number of African American soldiers to this isolated and desolate place. The area was always hot, dry, and extremely boring. Day after day went by and the slow extremely boring reality never changed.

Many soldiers were coming from overseas bases, during Vietnam, and were now at Laughlin. There were soldiers from cities like Detroit, Chi-town (Chicago), New York, and Philadelphia. Needless to say, Laughlin wasn't the cream of duty stations. People found creative ways to entertain themselves. It was like being in a social experiment for a study on unrest. The Base Commander wanted to head off the obvious unrest that was stirring on Laughlin before it got out of hand. The idea to put all these Black soldiers in the desert with nothing to do was going to be a problem.

The poem, *Del Rio Blues*, is about a meeting of hundreds of Black soldiers with the Base leadership to come up with a solution to stop the impending violence. The irony is that sometimes the most vocal representatives of the group are only trying to improve their personal circumstances. This was the case and nothing being talked about was going to improve anything. Because I felt it was a waste of time, I walked out. I didn't want to be a part of this fiasco and evidently some others felt as I did and opted to leave also.

I was the first to leave but the others left about the same time. Because we all left at approximately the same time and I moved first, the Office of Special Investigation targeted me as the ringleader and put me under investigation for something I didn't even know how to do. (I was twenty years old from a small town in Ohio.) This is how easily your life as a Black man can be turned upside down. Nothing came of it after several months because I wasn't leading anybody anywhere. It was scary, to say the least, to be constantly questioned about something that you weren't part of... the Del Rio Blues.

HERITAGE THOUGHTS

(2017)

There's our life and then there's our soul.

It's the soul that fires
life so each generation wants and does grow old.

The next remembers what
the last one told and because they now tell,

The next generation has a greater chance of doing well.

And a race of people grows old.

What if no one tells what they've been told?

The soul of the family will not grow old.

What will the grandkids have to tell if they've not been told

About bold old great, great grandpa

that bought himself back from being sold.

Those old pictures, in that ragged shoe box,

Has plenty people proudly posing, two rocking dreadlocks.

The son looks at his dad, with that smile, that says, 'Hey Pops

Is that my great,
great grandfather sporting them cool dreadlocks?'

Look at the pictures real hard; know what you'll see?

Some look just like my sisters and many look a lot like me.

Be glad you live in a family with old stories to tell;

That's the soul's life blood keeping the family alive and well.

Many times over, the family's old stories need told;

Told, over and over again, they should never grow old.

Told by those special ones
that have had the privilege of growing old

They've earned the right by and through sheer time--

Guiding the way of the family
with precious secrets of past times.

It's their turn to tell them. Then it will be mine

To ensure that there's not now, nor ever will there ever be

A broken or unattended family tree.

The "Tree of Life" was lost to mankind.

Lives got bent and twisted and the Garden of Eden's life tree

Was taken away by God for all eternity.

We became entangled in their "Tree of Lies";

A tree devoid of life's roots
that feeds the tree of our true lives.

Now, you no longer have to ask why--

The sacred truths about us,
must always and forever continue to survive.

They tell of the real greatness
that was once our free lives.

Boldly told

and passed down as the young truly become the old.

{101}

That's why we call each other brother,
'cause we kinfolk by pain--
Just not by the same mother or by the same last name.
This life made us brothers, as we weave history to tell
the truth that will keep our family trees strong
and our children doing well.

HERITAGE THOUGHTS

Everybody except African Americans came to this new land as immigrants. Immigrants free to marry other immigrants creating proud generational lineages from varying kinds of people. This eventually morphed into America and as the racial lines between immigrants from all over the globe blurred, we became Americans. Dutch, Irish, and German on the dad's side and Swedish on the mother's side; every combination of ethnicity acceptable from a European ethnicity standard happened. Many socially unaccepted unions also happened.

The unions between Blacks and Native Americans, with the varying immigrant combinations, did not produce the combined heritage names that made America so appealing to immigrants. Some immigrants sought to maintain their ethnic purity and forbid marriage outside of their ethnicity. They dreamed of one day visiting or returning to the country of their ancestors and wanting their heritage maintained. This pride in their ethnic heritages allowed families to proudly maintain family traditions, language, and ethnic pride and still be counted as Americans.

So, where do Black fathers find their racial pride morphing from slave to citizen? Our valued stories were mostly oral remnants of the life we were stolen from. Learning to read and write was expressly prohibited under penalty of death. Teaching our traditions in this new land, to remember our stories, to maintain our ethnic pride lead to punishment and even death. Yet, we still have our stories and ethnicity that's been passed down through our oral tradition.

At times, it might be more of a feeling than a known fact. The false scenario depicting our American existence has never rung true in our hearts. Our contributions to this society can be lied about but they can never be covered completely up. We have been too integral in this country's development. Many of our contributions were founded simply to make our life of servitude easier, our toil less taxing. Our contributions are not easily found in racist American history.

How do we as Black fathers raise our sons, so our sons will raise their sons with solid family values and ethnic pride? First, have yourself a big family hug. If no one else will give you a hug, give one to yourself. Black Man, no matter who you are or what you do, believe in and remember to focus on the next generation. Also, have a leading role in the small or larger village of your choosing. It does take a village to raise a child and a family. The generations that follow need you as a healthy self-aware life guide. Study to know who you are, what you stand for, and where you are going.

MAN SEED

(2020)

Tonight, the seed got sewn between her thighs

Sown in the early dawn of these two young people's and
sometimes old people's lives.

Playing family type games, not knowing they might win;

Neither can resist the thoughts
of making love over again and again.

What slick thing will you next try?

Will you tell her things that you know are pure lies?

Or will you dazzle her

With descriptions of the awesome beauty of her eyes?

Will you tell her of your beautiful budding future life

The two of you will share, if she bears and shares your life?

Did you recognize her need to be loved?

To find a secure home

To end the endless struggle, a woman feels,
when she goes it all alone.

Were these the words you've used over and over again?

That this... This you feel for her is more than just friends.

Did you tell her of your future,

And let her dare to dance with your dreams?

{105}

Of a lovely peaceful world where you worship her

and she can have all the wonderful things.

Was she your morning coffee, hot thighed and black?

A beautiful lady laying seductively on and across your lap.

Did you lighten her coffee, ever so slightly,
while she moaned to sweet whispered lies?

Did she moan or did she scream, as you added your warm
loving cream, to the length and width of her thighs?

She pants and she coos, hoping against hope,

This time she's not being fooled.

Lying there glistening, still steaming, smoking hot,

Struggling to know if she should believe in you--

Knowing she probably should not.

Patiently, she dates you, each and every day;

Now, she's trusting only in you, in her sweet,
loving special way.

Take it ever so slowly... smooth, never ever too fast,

Owning the love of this woman is a sweet,
slow and delicate task.

Was her love taken unjustly or
with sweet words and sweet lies?

Or taken sincerely, like you do when it is a true valentine?

The seeds you planted in passion are ripening just fine--

She can't help but wonder, will you be different this time?

Now, that the fruit has been picked
from her young loving vine,

Was there a seed also planted,
ripening in the soil of this man's mind?

Why not, where, when,
does the father seed get planted and defined?

The "Father Seed" that can ripen inside of him with time.

The rhythm of your bodies syncopated and aligned;

Hips slowly forward, halted, by soft collisions,
then slowed to a slow easy grind.

The man feels her willful surrender,
this woman feels like mine;

He halts for a moment and looks deeply into her eyes.

Unrealized in these moments his passion is flowing inside--

The lovers, they can't tell.

So many men feel confused with the slightest belly swell.

Something should stir inside him, as his, in her seed grows.

He seeks answers and solutions,
from those who really just don't know.

Reality groans.

It's hard for those so young
to pay the bills required for a decent home;

Once again, she'll be left all alone.

They argue more and start slamming doors;

Calling each other names and acting insane.

Now, he and you both know he cannot remain.

The police called and quickly they came.

Any domestic strife

a Black man knows, could cost him his life.

As a leaf does falling from a tree,

Blown by the wind, with lots of time;

He'll seek and find another loving, willing vine

To open with love's keys, honed from telling loving lies.

But you know what is insane?

I don't understand why none of these kids

Carry his last name.

MAN SEED

Black women bear our children and keep our lamps lit no matter how high or low we personally take them. The growing number of Black women being the breadwinners in Black homes disturbs me primarily because I don't want it to be true. I believe in the value of two parents in the home. We already have enough orchestrated processes to divide the Black family. Increasing the percentage of fatherless homes in our communities is not something Black men need to be helping with.

There also is an ever-increasing educational disparity growing between the Black Man and the Black Woman, another divisive reality. Many of our single women are choosing to become single mothers as they raise their families without the help of a man. This is becoming a trend in our culture. Is this a good thing or a bad thing? Who knows but it is a highly debated topic and 'Yes' might be winning over 'No'.

There is also a disparity in the number of available men to available women. The decision for many women is to move on with their family life plans outside of marriage.

Men having multiple babies with double-digit numbers of women is another reality of the Black community. This practice also has ongoing negative implications that can have irreversible social and psychological damage for generations. The scary part for the future is many of these children only carry the mother's family name, leading to the children not knowing from which bloodline they came. This I believe is one of the more disastrous trends in our culture. This makes our struggle as a cultural people even more difficult and we're doing it to ourselves because of an altered consciousness about family values.

What the *Man Seed* poem addresses is when or how does the concept of fatherhood take root in the man? And if so, where, what, and when? How did this baby daddy mentality happen? People use the term "Baby Daddy" with equivalency to "Father" or "Dad" and that is just wrong. Did someone or something make us forget life fundamentals? How important is it that this culturally destructive trend be reversed back to our historically strong family values that gave us stability in this unstable America? I, for one, think family values are essential to our survival and quality of life in our communities.

Now, Black Men, do your part to stop this negative "Man slide" before nothing about family life is sacred. Be a loving, caring, present man in your children's lives. Be the father, if you have a child or children whether you are married to the mother or not. If you believe raising your offspring is something that you have an obligation to do, you won't be so reckless during your times of pleasure and allow it to lead to pregnancy. Precious should be the babies and more precious should be their futures. They are our future after all. Black Man, they are your seeds and all of them need our guidance

I AIN'T GOT
NO SHINING STAR

(1976)

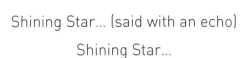

Shining Star... (said with an echo)
Shining Star...
Shining Star...

But I ain't got no shining star!

I got the earth for my theatre.
I got the sun and the moon for my lights.
I even got background music
but I ain't got no Shining Star!

Shining Star of ageless beauty
With a voice so sweet.
She calms the beast in me even while she sleeps.
Shining and shining and looking and finding
That which you mean to be.
A star you are and if you fall,
Know that patch of soft ground, I will be.

Shining Star, I will take you from the sky
and place you where my heart once was.
And your love will shine with mine
and through my eyes, a beam will flow,
For the whole wide world to know
that inside of me next to my heart.

A warm fire glows
For years to come, Shining Star--
We'll flow both day and night.
Until the night when we lie down together
and our African creation takes life.
We will teach her to care and respect herself
and we'll give her commandments to keep
In hopes that she grows to know and show,
The love that we tried to seek.

From this Shining Star, we'll grow tired
and know my promise I will keep:
I will lie down beside you in a bed of love
and love you while we sleep...
Shining Starrrrarrrr--
But I ain't got no Shining Star!

I AIN'T GOT
NO SHINING STAR

People want and need that person to help fulfill their dreams of life and family. They look forward to being a parent teaching their sons or daughters what they believe. For some people, having a loving mate and family is happiness. Before this journey can be followed, you need a mate that wants to take their journey with you; that love of a special person. Special, because they see you as equally wonderful, as you see them. He tells her of his story and she tells him of hers. They dream, listen, share, and have a wonderful time doing for each other.

Many people go their entire life looking for that someone their heart and soul connects with. They pass up many wonderful opportunities because it's not what they've envisioned in their heart. The dream of loving one day that perfect love can lead you to many disastrous relationships. As you mature, you will realize that often what you desire most in your loved one may be very superficial qualities that will fade with time. That wonderful person may not be so wonderful when you actually get to know them.

When you find your perfect person, the one that meets all of what you think a mate should be, it would be sound advice to spend time making sure their life's desires and goals match what you want them to be for you.

I've found that the first tragedy in many young people's lives happens when they choose their mate. Up until then, their lives have been simple and mostly good. Their parents took wonderful care of them. They graduate high school and go straight to college. Graduate college and are awarded a wonderful employment opportunity. Now, they are in their late twenties and are ready to start a family. They pick what seems like the perfect person to them. For numerous reasons, the marriage or love affair ends in a broken heart. In this poem, a shining star is someone you can dream with. It's the person you trust, as you trust yourself. It's their commitment that they want the reality you are offering. It meets their dream picture and yours. Shining Stars are not always just the person you'll marry and grow old with. A friend can be a Shining Star. When you need them, they are there for you, just as you will be for them.

BECAUSE SHE
RECOGNIZED MY PAIN

(1990)

I loved someone that I didn't even know--

There was no magic.

We ate no dinner, no dancing.

Words just weren't important.

Yet, as her hands caressed my shoulder, I felt released--

Released from the logic of the loss of you.

For a moment, it just didn't matter

What went wrong between you and I.

I knew I tried everything, maybe I tried too much.

Now, I stand on that one second in my life

When my life stopped by an unknown command--

Never to move again until I understand.

Then, I met my stranger.

We didn't dance nor dine.

We simply sat and talked, and the world moved again.

I grew scared, I wanted to believe it was you.

Yet, still her simple kindness
released me moment by moment

and my inner world spins again.
Darkness prevailed all about.
My lips followed the path of faces
and caresses needed only be warm.
Fingers counted one after the other
As if that mattered.
Nothing said.
Nothing explained.
But I believe again, and humanity survives
because she recognized my pain.

BECAUSE SHE
RECOGNIZED MY PAIN

As a young man moving through the world on your own, life events will trigger internal responses that must be dealt with. One of many is heartache. Heartache can be in the forefront of your life, plaguing your every thought throughout the days, weeks, months, and yes and even years. Heartache can also be subtle; causing you to trust less or follow a path that is simply unfulfilling.

Whatever the degree of the pain is that has your life off-kilter, sometimes it helps to meet that compatible stranger to spark your healing. Someone that sees your good and enjoys sharing their good while helping you get yourself back together. There's a sweetness in this that the wanderers of life recognize. If you are a good man who just has the blues in his life on some level, there will be that special stranger that meets you where you are and shares with you their pleasures and their joys. They will do this simply because for some reason, helping you find your way, brings them joy.

CONFUSION

(1980)

The sweet sounds soften my heart.

The tears fall.

Lovely is the day,

I feel my lost-ness and yet, see my way.

I follow myself, myself before and myself now as I exist,

This is the wisdom of my eternity.

Yet, my internal war causes pain.

My mind's ancestors and slave realities refuse to unite:

One loves the day and one loves the night.

I stand torn and no one sees,

For the battle rages only inside of me.

My hair is me; my skin, I am my power--

I know who rules.

One side dies a slave of my intellect.

I shall cut off this side's world

and today I live a different one.

I am new birth;

Borne of a new son.

I'll master my dreams,

The images of my mind will change all things.

Reality groans. My kids go without a decent home.

One side, the teeter-totter rises.

Teardrops form on my fists

and drop upside their heads.

CONFUSION

America struggles because she is composed of immigrants that became Americans, little by little. Rules for the creation of a nation were made to keep power sequestered in one group, while stingily relinquishing select freedoms to others as specific situations arose...confusion. Different groups entered America under different rules of engagement and the rules that bound Black people prohibited us from playing...confusion.

Whereas, some immigrant groups arrived here as laborers and explorers, we arrived here as slaves. Thus, the pigmentation of our skin was saddled with strategically placed lies about our nature and culture which created a uniquely intense resistance to our liberation and progress. This presented Black folks with an especially unique uphill battle to the promises espoused by the constitutional covenant of this country. Bring us your poor and huddled masses, blah, blah, blah...confusion.

Any understanding of our struggle or actions begins with understanding one fact: We must love ourselves. We must also embrace that while our history is riddled with particularly harsh obstacles, our present is full of unprecedented opportunities for community healing and progress. If you are personally living in a manner that is destructive to yourself, your community, or your loved ones, then you must change the way you live. Understand that today you have the character to do so and your reality is shaped by your guidance.

Overcoming the external struggles that we still face will require us to truly operate as neighbors and as individuals submitting to the natural laws that govern the creation of community and culture. Our frustrations cannot be our guiding light. Frustration offers no guidance, only confusions.

BLUE LIGHT CHANDELIER

(2010)

Forced from the home, I knew so well--

Where I planted trees, flowers

and some things of which I cannot tell.

Multiple voices and noises, that I knew well.

Noises of home that made my heart swell;

This was my home.

I don't need to ring the doorbell.

Clanging pots and clanging pans;

Kids pushing and shoving,
each growing to be a really fine man.

Then, life went off course

when the noises I heard were those of divorce.

Now, when I put my head to the ground,

I cannot hear my once contented family sounds.

I, now, hear the muffled
and loud noises of speeding motor bikes

that waken me unexpectedly, in the middle of the night--

'Cause now my home is on a main site

just down the street from a busy traffic light.

Just as I again fall asleep,

the police pull someone over--

Inviting me to share

In their midnight game of pullover

and put your hands in the air.

Sometimes, I just get their blue light chandelier

flipping on my walls at its steady pace--

'Cause the police chase ended right
in front of this non-family place.

I count the blue flashes as the night passes by;

They lull me to sleep like a dangerous lullaby.

Where are they going so fast?

Blasting loud pipes as they pass.

Silence visits but it does not stay;

there's new noises as the speeders
and cruisers with boom boxes

go on their way.

How did your life get here and how long will I stay?

Everyone says leave there before it's your blood

Next time in your driveway.

You're living life to close to your old past.

Living your ancient life

Before you had children, a wife, and became a dad.

How can this be?

You wonder. I wonder, What happened to me?

One minute, I'm planning what next should we do.

Then, court becomes reality

and you and I are really through...

And the blue light chandelier flashes

in my life another night.

BLUE LIGHT CHANDELIER

Divorce can be tragic event that occurs far too often in our communities. Divorce can take away, a little, a lot, or all of your prosperity but you still have to have a place to stay. Living now on a main thoroughfare for the first time in my life is a unique experience. The traffic light was just the right distance from my house and the speeding cars that got caught in their speed trap usually landed exactly in front of my picture window.

Every night, I'm now treated to the blue light atop the police car bouncing off my ceiling like a chandelier in a fancy club that didn't require a tuxedo. Don't talk about the noise from the crotch rockets speeding by at 100 plus miles per hour, scaring me to death as I slept. They are so sudden and loud. Forget about the expensive bass speakers that boomed, boomed, boomed as they crept by on twenty sixes with everyone slightly leaning just enough for coolness. The transient people that wandered into my yard from time to time were harmless but very odd.

These experiences prompted this poem. I look back on these times and smile, but I don't ever want to do them again.

YOUR EYES

(2020)

Standing on the edge of someone else's life,
Looking over their edge only with your eyes.
Realizing your eyes will not be enough to see their reality,
Can I borrow your eyes so I can see what you see?
I'll even slide down for a closer look.
And being closer only intensifies,
The reality of my need for your eyes.

Maybe, I'll just listen as time passes;
So, I can understand better what you say.
Can I borrow your ears?
I fear, I am not hearing, as I listen;
Although, I do try.

Standing on the edge of someone else's life.
Too far away to see, too far away to hear
and words only matter if you understand them, as they do.
The clock ticks, the never stopping clock tocks.
Somehow, we again start to talk.
Realizing we were so far apart, with our own good intentions;
Intentions that seem at that time, to be enough.

Now I know they were not

Because you let me have... your eyes.

YOUR EYES

Relationships often go wrong and neither party can really tell you why. A long time passes and occasionally you wonder about that person, that at one time you loved. More time passes and from time to time, they come back to mind. Nothing overtly bad happened. You just grew further and further apart until you both agreed to end the relationship.

You've probably tried various ways to understand each other but to no avail. Maybe one day you will be lucky enough to meet that person again and have an opportunity to talk, with neither of you now having any agenda, except to satisfy your curiosity. It's just a chance you can take advantage of. Each of you puts your cards on the table and you realize, you just weren't hearing each other. Each of you were caught in your own reality and couldn't, or chose not to, hear the desires of your mate. The poem, *Your Eyes*, speaks to that reality.

A WORD TO PASTORS

(2020)

A man of God sitting under a tree

that shades the driveway to the temple of peace.

He was filled with pride as
all his parishioners happily passed by

and many stopped to share just a brief, "Hi".

His robes of white pressed just right;

A beautiful gold cross laid cross
his chest just laying perfectly on a lovely red crest.

His life felt so right all his days and all through his nights.

He was very content just
to be a Holy Christian sitting under his tree

that shaded the driveway to his temple of peace.

Life so simple as all who walked
by on the way to their lives stopped or waved just to say, "Hi".

No day was particular, never any reason for despair;

He'd rise early, shower, dress and carefully comb his hair.

The tree that shaded the driveway
and the temple of peace were always there.

This day was like most: the gold cross on his chest the one
that laid perfectly on the red crest with the robes
of white that were always pressed just right.

He put the cross in his mouth, thinking
of a Christian joke when all of a sudden, he started to choke.

And there for a moment standing there
he was struggling to just catch enough air.

His friend was there and rushed
to him when he saw his despair.

Lord, Why? Why did you almost take my life with the cross I
bear in my robes of white that were always pressed just right
and showed best when the gold cross
that laid against the red crest?

I could not breath nor expand my chest.

Have you no eyes? Can you not see

you were choked by your precious gold cross

Not by anything of Me.

I gave you My love for all man;

But you turned my words with your own tithing plan

and your proof with tongues that come from man.

You are My guiding hands,

Now your arms are too short to touch your fellow man.

From the so high place you've chosen to stand,

Altering my words to gain your control of economic plans.

You know I'm the spirit of love.

I sent no pictures of Jesus from up above.

No list of those not worthy,

Works were never part of My spiritual journey.

I gave you the voice of the Holy Spirit.

Now, all I see is your desire and greed
that you are calling a message from Me.

My spirit dwells not in the earthly ways
you talk about to collect your pay

To Me, My anointed, you've lost the way.

You keep trying to sell a message of prosperity
from My sacred place;

My unseen temple that I died to save.

The cross that choked you and held My hands,

Was of your making and not part of My plan.

A WORD TO PASTORS

Sometimes, I get confused with this thing called prosperity ministry. Huge churches get larger and more powerful because of the generosity of the tithers and really for no other reason. They would have you believe that their growth is entirely due to God's anointing on their church for being a vanguard of His word. Oftentimes, their vanguardship is lacking spiritual worthiness but as long as the tithing continues by those looking for prosperity, how do you tell the difference?

They need planes and multiple fine homes and all the other material things that they promise to the followers if they do not rob the church and God of tithes. I mean no disrespect to pastors and I do love the Lord, but this is on my heart. The more given, the more they want. Being comforted behind the sentiment that only God can judge them is beyond my capability.

I need spiritual guidance and I truly believe that the world could use some spiritual guidance especially now and that is my daily prayer. The original title to this poem was Pimping Pastors but that name didn't sit well with my upbringing. This poem is not a condemnation of the ministry as a whole. It is desirable that no man be blindly followed, especially if you're following from a prosperity position that will elevate your life if you are just faithful to the tithing teachings of the church.

SELF-APPOINTED-YOU

(2020)

Can I breathe just this one time,
without you trying to have me hurt

For committing no crime?

I'm just working my job or just enjoying my free time.

I'm taking a simple walk in my neighborhood,
with beauty for miles;

Beauty that takes my breath away and just makes me smile.

A walk to let my eyes enjoy the accomplishments of my life,

If only for a brief while.

As I live and breathe, it's nice to take
a deep breath just because I'm really pleased.

My tranquility suddenly leaves, all beauty is still there.

Because the self-appointed-you intrudes
with your beliefs that are not exactly fair.

You need answers because you don't like my skin;

You don't like my hair.

The you who cannot accept that success lets me
too live equal or maybe even better than you.

I just may be the last step to internet shopping,
where you buy with pride;

I make your desires arrive
without you having to going outside.

You click and then I get paid to drive,
making the desires of your life arrive.

My work takes me outside;

Many times, it takes me where
the self-appointed-you resides.

With only twisted racist beliefs,

you start texting to your neighbors in a collective
of racist tweets.

Tweets about a black man wondering around on our streets--

And I can't breathe because explaining
my existence lets you treat me like a thief.

The police come and they explain, in these times,
being on your personal streets is not a crime;

But illegally detaining someone will get you arrested
and you could do time.

What about the self-appointed-you? Who makes me late
and wastes everyone's time.

Making black and white American strangers all start to cry

because for no reason...I had to die.

From injuries sustained only because you lied and screamed,

The lives lost from your judgmental schemes
that got me choked because of American racist themes.

I'm jogging. I love to run.

I love doing normal exercise things out in the sun.

As my skin starts to glow
and the sweat runs down my face, my breath starts to blow.

I need more air as I quicken my pace
and my stride starts to flow.

My muscles flex, my muscles swell,
I'm just putting in the good work.

Why can't you just see that? Why can't you tell?

I'm through for today. Now, I desired
that my workout end in my shower;

Not arguing or answering nosey questions
so you can feel empowered:

Questions saved for homeowners who
you don't know or don't look like you.

The ones that make you feel uncomfortable until
you question them about what they do.

Now! It's ok, this one can stay;

He's a doctor or he or she is famous in some notable way.

The self-appointed you strikes again.

You just wanted to protect your neighborhood
from the color of my skin.

Now, you think your apology ladened with stereotypical lies,

Will give you a chance to somehow be a part of our lives.

I only want friends and neighbors

That don't try to control how much or how long
I can breathe and survive.

That don't play from that sacred, racist,
scared, deck of cards,

Just because they saw a black man run past their yard.

That hateful card from your hate filled deck
that you played that day

Could have cost me injury, embarrassment, even life,
before I could explain.

Were you really that frightened, confused or dismayed,

That I'm here just like you because of what I'm paid?

Whether you're at the bottom in America
or all the way to the top,

You know and I know assumed social privilege
makes you drink from the same racists American pot.

Is it really asking a lot

To walk in my neighborhood and not get racially stopped?

Not have my life turned into a living hell

every time a self-appointed you starts to yell.

Yes, I breathe just fine when I'm given my respect.

How would you feel if my fight for
my equality put my foot or knee on your neck?

SELF-APPOINTED-YOU

The internet is filled with white American citizens believing that they are owed an explanation because they feel they want one. This is being coined as a symptom of Systemic Racism.

The unbelievable part is when they call the police without any reason other than the person is Black. The police respond and support their irrational perspective that somehow this Black person should explain, to the satisfaction of everyone that is wondering, why you're on this street. Any reasonable person being questioned about being in the neighborhood where they live should absolutely be offended. Except not totally cooperating can cost this Black person their life, freedom (arrest), or bodily harm. If this atrocity imposed on the citizen is found to have been done in error, apologies are not enough restitution for the multiple kinds of damage this individual had to endure because of white systemic racist beliefs that stem from nothing more than how they think about Black people, especially Black men.

I cannot change the reflexes of systemic racists. No matter how hard I try, the theory of integration has not addressed this issue. Black people have been productive citizens and fought for this country. We are no better or generally no worse than any other race of people. I can make a case that racism is an institutional reflex that litigation and legislation have been able to impact but not correct and eliminate. It is up to the person that has this racist institutional reflex to govern themselves. They have to realize that systemic racism won't help them flourish in life.

Made in the USA
Columbia, SC
30 September 2020

21734877R00088